All Scripture references taken from the KJV of the Holy Bible, unless otherwise indicated.

The Emptiers: *Thieves of Darkness*

Dr. Marlene Miles

Freshwater Press 2024

ISBN: 978-1-963164-26-8

Paperback Version

Copyright 2024, Dr. Marlene Miles

All rights reserved. No part of this book may be reproduced, distributed, or transmitted by any means or in any means including photocopying, recording or other electronic or mechanical methods without prior written permission of the publisher except in the case of brief publications or critical reviews.

Table of Contents

Emptied 4
Introduction 5
Void & Without Form 8
Replenish the Earth 11
Restoration Power 12
Don't Want You to Have It 14
The Emptier 18
Where's My Money? 22
Emptiers Eat Time 31
Emptying the Nest 34
They Want You Broke 37
The Spiritual Realm 42
Stolen Parts 47
Emptier Items 52
Sex 55
Stealing Prayers 70
Scrambled 73
Consummate Thieves 76
Recovery 79
Prayer Points 82
Dear Reader 95
Other books by this author 96

The Emptiers
Thieves of Darkness 1

Emptied

In the beginning, God created the heaven and the Earth.

Genesis 1:1

and the earth was without form, and void; and darkness was upon the face of the deep. And the Spirit of God moved upon the face of the waters.

Genesis 1:2

Introduction

The thieves of darkness who come to steal from the saints of God are *emptiers, wasters, swallowers*, and *devourers*.

When it comes to empty, there are only a few good kinds of empty. The empty Cross is a sign of victory for our Christ and the Body. The empty tomb because the Lord Jesus is arisen, Hallelujah! The empty grave is the sign that death has lost its power and the saints of God do not go on to glory until the Lord says so, not before.

- Lord, let every grave, every pit dug for me, become the resting spot for the one who dug it, and not me. Let me escape as a bird, in the Name of Jesus.

And as Dr. Myles Munroe taught, the person who is empty because they gave out all of the gifts that God put in them for mankind; that is, you fulfilled purpose and reached destiny that is a good kind of empty. There are few other kinds, unless we consider if **hell** were empty because **all people** got saved and were out of reach of the devil that would be good.

However, it would be bad if evil entities and powers were no longer locked away where they should be because evil human agents and ignorant souls have summoned them up from hell. And they not only have no way to put them back, they have no power to do it, because by summoning them, they have compromised their own authority and power that God had given them by being born man, in the Earth.

Of the most distressing things are the empty wallet, or the empty purse. As well we hate the empty life, the empty suit, the empty barrel, and the barren womb. In this book we will find out how empty things that we don't want to be empty, or *void* got that way, and what we can do about it.

Void & Without Form

In the beginning God created the Heaven and the Earth. The Earth was without form, and void; and darkness was upon the face of the deep and the Spirit of God moved upon the face of the waters. Verse 2 is especially interesting because do we think that God made something void, that He made it in darkness and without form? No, the Bible says that the Word of God will not return to Him void, but that Word will return to God having completed what God sent it out to do.

Since God made the Heavens and the Earth and all that is in it by **speaking**, then He made it all with His Word. His Word is that which will not return to Him void.

As God said, **Let us make man in our own image and likeness,** He said that with His Word. God made man a certain way, He didn't make man void, without form, or lacking anything. Man was created perfect and perfectly, before the Fall. Then sin began to be expressed in our DNA. Sin can never express itself as God, therefore once sin entered in so did imperfection.

God created the Heavens and the Earth and He created them perfectly. they were not void, they were not in darkness or without form when God created them, with His Word that performs.

So, what happened between God creating the Heaven and the Earth to Verse 2 where there is this void?

You guessed it – the devil comes not but to steal, kill & destroy. Scorched Earth is courtesy of the devil. All grinchy, the devil destroyed, stole, and or corrupted probably everything that God made. You can tell by the way he's after man to tear up man and mankind, that he'd try to tear up the Earth and everything God made, as if he was having a tantrum.

The devil left the Earth in a place of void, so that makes him an *emptier*. To be empty means to be void. An *emptier* is one who empties or exhausts, wears it out, corrupts it. Drains it. Makes it void and in the case of Earth, *without form.*

Replenish the Earth

If God said, **Replenish**, meaning to fill it, then the devil would do the opposite, he'd try to empty it.

God made man perfectly but because the Earth was void and without form, this is why God told them *to be fruitful and multiply*, and God also said for them to REPLENISH the Earth. He didn't say plenish it, which means to equip, to fill, stock, or resupply. God said, REPLENISH it, which means at some point it had been plenished. **Replenish** would therefore mean to make it like it was before or make it the way it was supposed to be – the way it was when God originally made it.

Restoration Power

Saints of God, not only is that quite an assignment, but it is also quite a testament and a testimony to what God imbued in man that man would be <u>able</u> to replenish, that is, properly restore something that <u>God had made,</u> back to its original form.

That's why the Psalmist asks: *Who is man that thou art mindful of him?* That is a question to ponder: Who is man who can put his hands to something that God had made and in essence create or recreate what God had already made? Furthermore, besides being able to destroy the works of the devil, we can also REVERSE the damage that the devil has done. I know this because GOD said, **Be fruitful and multiply**, and GOD also said, **REPLENISH the Earth**. To me, that means Earth itself, all of Earth and everything that is in it.

By the great inventions of man, inventions of convenience, we have created air pollution and assaulted the ozone layer. It seems that man has done the opposite of what God said to do. That means that man has been listening to the enemy all this time---.

Whoa – saints of God.

Or it could mean that man has done little to nothing and the devilish entropy of the devil to tear up things and empty things, render them useless and void has persisted for eons.

Woe! Saints of God. We need to wake up!

Don't Want You to Have It

Ever meet a kid who is forever wanting the toy the other kid has, just because the other kid has it? They may not even want the toy, but they just don't want the other kid to have it.

This is a spirit. That's an *emptier spirit*. They don't want someone else to have something or to have anything, really. This behavior, this spirit is not relegated to only children; adults are rampant with this attitude, as well.

I knew someone that if they think I have anything, especially money – they want it from me. I've shared this story before, and it goes like this: If I find a quarter while walking along on the sidewalk, that person will find a reason to need that quarter before the end of that day. If they think I have something of monetary value, they want it. That is a *spirit*, it is the *spirit* of the *emptier*.

You may have met people like that and hopefully steering clear of them. Those are the people who can't stand to see you have anything. Do not tell them about things you have, especially new things. Don't tell them you have a new car, house, friend--, boyfriend girlfriend—nothing. But especially do not tell them of things you have of monetary value. They will be eaten up by what looks to be jealousy, but they take it to a whole other level, because if the *spirit of the emptier* is working in them, they will stop at nothing trying to drain every good thing, and all the valuable things from your life. They don't want you to have it; they want it.

So, I say again, stop putting all your business on social media. The *spirit* of the *emptier* is looking for a life to empty.

Oh, you may think I'm taking this too far. I'm not. You may argue that the people on social media don't know you, don't know where you live--, they don't know anything about you. I beg to differ. They know everything about you that you post online. In addition, many things are spiritually discerned, and if they are into the dark arts, they can get info on you from *monitoring spirits*, and *familiar spirits*, for example. It's demonic, and for nefarious purposes, but they can get it--, unless you are prayed up. If you are posting online all day, chances are pretty good that you are not prayed up, but some are.

Now, when it comes to ripping you off, they don't have to live in your vicinity. Folks, this stuff is done in the spirit and not by the Spirit of God. These thieves of which I write are thieves of darkness. If you are out there broadcasting your business online, you are in essence putting your star out there in their dark world, so you know your star is going to be bright. If you don't have proper spiritual protection, an *emptier* can just come and get it.

There is not just a dark web; there is a dark world, a dark kingdom and the thieves of which I write inhabit that world.

The Emptier

The *emptiers,* no matter what they themselves have, they don't want to see you with anything. They want to take you from grace to disgrace. They want to take you from a place of honor to dishonor. If they take you from success to failure, they are happy. From wealth to poverty, that's their goal; they don't want you to have anything.

> The kingdom of heaven suffereth violence and the violent take it by force, (Matthew 11:12b).

When you've finally had enough, you realize that things needed for your life and godliness – spouse, marriage, family, children, are being taken from you, or have been taken from you that you have to take them back by force. We are not fighting people, we are not warring against flesh and blood; we must take back whatever has been stolen from us in the spirit, by spiritual warfare.

Emptiers empty good things from peoples' lives, even good people. *Emptiers* don't come to kill; their intention is only to empty. They really come to steal more than to kill or destroy.

You might meet mean girls – mean boys, mean men, mean women-- who want to take what you have are motivated by and influenced by, and empowered to do so by the *emptier spirit.* You've met the type – they will take what you have and smash it just because they don't want you to have it. I'm talking about spiritual entities, but it will manifest in the natural some kind of way; unfortunately, some have been married to those who will take or smash your things. Yelling at that person and telling them that they are an *emptier* is not how you handle this. This must be managed spiritually, in prayer.

Like the devil messing up the perfect Earth that was intact when he landed here, falling from Heaven, like lightning, that is how the *emptiers* tear up things. Earth was perfect. God had made it, so you know it was perfect. But he turns it void and without form because God gave the Earth to man and the devil doesn't want man to have Earth or enjoy it.

The devil did all this damage, but without a human body the devil has no authority in the Earth. Earth wasn't made for the devil; it was made for man. Therefore, he did all this through evil human agents and corrupting the elements to be destructive instead of helpful to man as they were originally designed by God.

The highest heavens belong to the lord, but the earth he has given to mankind.
(Psalm 115:16 NIV)

Where's My Money?

I have heard more than one testimony of a person saying they had a dream, or they went to Heaven and God showed them all the wealth and riches that He had for them on Earth. You may have heard preachers say that there will be so much treasure in Heaven once we get there and we will see what we could have had, but didn't have while on Earth.

Surely the enemy knows that if you are sent to Earth as a priest, and a king you should have wealth. So, he has juxtaposed himself between you and

God and especially between you and the money and wealth that God has earmarked for you.

Enter the *emptiers*.

Once this emptying has started by the *spirit of the emptier*, victims of the emptiers have a hard time prospering.

The only way out of it is GOD, through Christ Jesus. You must put on Christ, and be <u>fully</u> in the Lord, who will deliver you from this.

These can't be lovey dovey prayers; there are occasions for that, but unless people really deal with these *emptiers*, spiritually –they will remain poor. We are not praying that the Lord will save the *emptiers*, they are demons. We are praying **against** demons, they cannot be saved, they cannot be redeemed and to paraphrase Evangelist Sarah, *I am not going to pray for the*

devil to repent.
https://www.youtube.com/watch?v=ooP_EAlewkA

This is spiritual work that must be done, in the spirit. These are not bank robbers—that you fend off with guns, the *emptiers* are spiritual entities. This is going to take warfare prayer, unless you don't think that stealing is violence. It may also take fasting. The only way out of the clutches of *emptier spirits* is in God, and to fully put on Christ. It will take prayer, spiritual warfare, fasting and some **violence**.

There are many variations. What they do and how they do it is entirely up to their evil imagination or how they have been taught to empty the lives, benefits, blessings, and finances of others. Or what the evil demon that they have accessed from the pit of hell, is telling them at that time.

The dark kingdom has studied you since your birth, or before. They have seen exactly what the best weapon is to use against you, how to implement it and when to do it. Yes, through *monitoring* and *familiar spirits* a plan has been devised and is probably waiting for the right day. This is a clue as to how weapons are really formed against you. Like a slow cooker, simmering slowly over time with plans to put you in a pressure cooker.

I am of the mind that if someone tells you that they are jealous of you— they are. It's a statement of fact, not a compliment. Get prayed up – even if these are your friends, real or fake, or even family members. Get prayed up, stay prayed up. Not everyone who is jealous of you will tell you… get prayed up, stay prayed up.

Do not think that jealousy and the *emptier spirit* will only come through distant friends or associates. No, it will come from close people. Do not think if you're a woman that only other women will be jealous of you. No, anyone, even men can be jealous of you. In the world women are provoked to be jealous of one another. It is a devil tactic to keep women from talking to one another, to keep them separated from one another so rogue men who are full of *lust*, polygamy, the devil, and *game* can continue to run their game on women.

But some of you can attest that you've met your share of men who are jealous of you, and you're a woman. You were not expecting that at all, were you? Some of those people you were actually dating them, and it never dawned on you that the person you are dating, or married to is jealous of you, or competing with you. But there it is. Unless this is resolved, it may mean the end of that relationship, but it can answer a lot of questions as to why the relationship was as difficult or as rocky as it was.

A jealous person will never have your best interest at heart. A jealous person will never promote you. A jealous person is full of a work of the flesh, as well as other *spirits*. If you let one demon in, they act as a butler and open the door for as many other demons as possible.

If the Holy Spirit is not in that soul there is a lot of space for lesser, evil, flesh demons to squat in that soul. The first evil demon in is going to be standing at that door and opening it a lot. One or both people full of flesh will sour that relationship, making it no fun to be in. Further, God won't be in it if it is overrun with flesh, so there will be no protection when a jealous person is influenced by an *emptier* to be competitive and bring the other down as if they are in a competition. Neither will

God be in this when the one who feels oppressed retaliates. God also won't be there to stop the *emptier spirit* from running amok because there is no protection in that house so either or both people could be run into the ground.

Emptiers – the spiritual entities, and their evil human counterparts are planning to get their blessings from you, by stealing from you, rather than from God. Because they are not in line to receive from God. They are not candidates to receive from God, and they surely can't steal from God. The Bible says in Malachi 3, *Will a man rob God?* Nowhere does it say that Satan took anything from God. The Word further says that no one can take you out of God's hand. So, if you are not in God's hand, we must deduce that you jumped out of it, yourself, or were lured away by the devil.

So, we must conclude that God is robbery-proof, except for man. *Who is man that God has His mind full of him, this man that can sin and can also rob God?* **And, yet He still loves us.**

It's amazing; His Grace.

These demons, do they *need* blessings? God gives us things for our life and for our godliness. *Well*, demons don't have godliness or flesh bodies because they are spirit, but since they employ or deploy evil human agents, those agents are either paid or are enticed to believe that they will be paid. Money and other perks are involved whenever bribery, even spiritual bribery is used. So, the devil and his demons don't need *things and stuff* for themselves, but they need *things and stuff* to put in the hands of his evil human agents. It's a racket, isn't it?

And, they get that *stuff* by stealing it from God's people. These evil *spirits* don't need what they are taking from you, **and** they don't want YOU to have it. These are hallmark traits of an *emptier*.

Don't let it be you, that they are emptying, *please*.

- Lord, in the Name of Jesus, let the *Emptiers* of my father's house, die, in the Name of Jesus.

Emptiers Eat Time

Emptiers eat time. Jacob was 20+ years in Laban's house—running from his brother, Esau, originally. Then he was delayed by Laban who kept changing this and that, about the terms of Jacob being there. Laban changed Jacob's salary. Jacob was working fiendishly while at Laban's place, but having an *emptier spirit,* Laban wanted to take Jacob's earnings. This would have made it look as though Jacob wasn't even working; that is a hallmark of the *emptier spirit.* Laban finagled with the promise of which woman Jacob could have for a wife. Laban tried his best to empty Jacob, but God said, **NO**.

The only way to get out of the clutches of an *emptier* is in GOD.

Emptiers will try to tie you down to one place doing something you never planned to do or should be doing, or you weren't planning to do long term, as Jacob was at Laban's house. He was only supposed to be at Laban's house for a few days. An *emptier* will tie you down and drain you. That gives me the evil image of a captive tied to a table and being embalmed—to be as one who is dead, while still alive. The *emptier spirit* will try to suck the life out of you; don't let it.

- Lord, in the Name of Jesus, my money if it's tied to a tree, buried anywhere, hidden anyplace, wherever the *emptiers* have hidden or stored it--, my money -- jump out and locate me, in the Name of Jesus.

- Any power that wants to keep me poor, somersault and die, in the Name of Jesus.
- *Emptiers* who have robbed me of my children by contaminating them, return my children to me, and be scattered by the power in the Blood of Jesus.

Emptying the Nest

Emptiers will steal people's children, Emptying the nest, but not in a good way, putting parents to shame. This makes it look as though the parents didn't raise their children correctly. The *emptier* can somehow change the kid's hearts. You've seen kids start out so good but later turn bad? The *emptier* has turned them into something unrecognizable. This is the evil work of the *emptiers*, emptying out the goodness and natural affection that was in your child. *Where has that love, and affection gone?* I've heard more than a few parents lament that their child had changed to such a degree that they didn't even recognize them anymore.

Instead of blaming it on another kid, or another person, or the alleged bad company your child is now keeping, recognize that this is spiritual and needs prevailing, relentless, violent prayer and fasting to snatch that child back from the *emptiers* before it's too late.

GO. GET. YOUR. KID.

We do not war against flesh and blood. If you have a child, whether you've ever done spiritual warfare or not—it is time to learn and to do it!

- Evil-hearted, revenge-minded people who knowingly or blindly wished evil on me, or my children, you're an *emptier* and a *waster,* you need to scatter, scatter, in the Name of Jesus.

Emptiers are demonically charged and can make people get rid of their own blessings, push their own blessings away with their own hands. Yes, the devil and his entourage are *emptiers*. But people can be emptiers toward other people, as well; we've talked about evil human agents.

But every *emptier* is not necessarily an evil human agent. Knowingly or unknowingly the devil has made man into an *emptier*, when he has convinced man to do the opposite of God's command to **replenish**. Has man even realized this yet? That by his own hand he is causing loss and destruction in the Earth and possibly in his own life, as well. That is in the natural, but in the spiritual realm we must look deeper.

- Lord, let that not be the case for us, in the Name of Jesus.

They Want You Broke

Emptiers are behind bad things that happen in people's lives. They are behind bad dreams that people have.

Other signs of *emptiers* in a person's life are:

- Seeing dead people in the dream.
- Eating in the dream, especially with dead relatives.
- Snakes in the dream.
- Spiritual marriages, spirit spouses.
- Sex in the dream.

Emptiers are behind incurable diseases, those that make you spend every dollar you have seeking a cure. They don't get a cure, but people are still alive, and suffering, and afflicted. Yet, they live.

The woman with the issue of blood in the New Testament had seen many physicians and spent all she had, yet she still had the issue, and she was still alive. She was frail, drained, sick – and broke, but still alive. That disease was an *emptier*, or it was sent by an *emptier*.

And, it took JESUS to heal it. We need Jesus every day. Amen.

- *Emptiers* can be responsible for business losses.
- Broken marriages.
- Everything that costs money… it is a thief.
- Sexual perversions.
- Drug abuse.

- Alcoholism.

Look at those last three, sexual perversion, alcoholism, drug abuse – those are things that you find people doing who are living the party life. So, a person doesn't have to be visibly sick to be a victim of the *emptier spirit*. **A fool and his money will soon party** is what I say. But we know that long term, sexual perversion, alcoholism and drug abuse are diseases, and most definitely can lead to *other* diseases, so then whatever money was not spent on the party life, being a barfly or nightclubber indulging in ritual sex such as one-night stands, the rest of that person's money can be consumed by medical treatments trying to get well, or to hopefully be cured of the ailments that come along with that lifestyle.

The *emptier* is a thief of the darkness. That doesn't mean that it only comes at night, it means that it is spawned from the dark kingdom, the kingdom of the devil. It is a thief, and emptying is a form of thievery. There is a demonic power to them, a demonic anointing to all this stuff, so you have to be spiritual to counter it, to stop it, and to get your deliverance from it.

Emptiers are responsible for:

- Evil call.
- Evil instructions.
- Distracting *spirits*. – if you can't focus, how will you succeed--, at anything?
- Trouble reading the Bible, worshiping the Lord, listening to the Word of God, or praying.
- Introject: things moving in the body, is from these *emptier spirits*.
- *Monitoring spirits*
- Automatic failure mechanism.
- Self-sabotage.

Spiritually, a victim or evil agent is being manipulated by some powers which are bent on making him or her broke, making sure that human looks like or remains a failure. They are sent to take all the joy and beauty out of their lives. To make them lose the abundant life that Jesus came that we should have. This is so demonic, yet powerful that these *spirits* can lead a person to self-sabotage, lead them to self-destruct, to destroy good things from their own lives, with their own hands.

The Spiritual Realm

You know that life is spiritual. The spiritual realm is as real as the physical one that we are in.

In the spiritual realm, which actually controls the physical world, when you pray, as a saint of God, your prayer may become a powerful weapon against the enemy. It may become Fire… especially when you are praying, Fire, and calling down Fire as Elijah did. It may become a sword, if you are using the Word of God which is the Sword of the Spirit. It may become a knife, or any dangerous weapon to destroy things and entities that have been programmed against you in the spirit world. So, you must pray and you should pray violent prayers because the *emptiers* are not playing with you.

As said, they didn't come to kill, they came to steal, but who wants to be ripped off? No one. They don't care if you're saved, they don't care if you're alive, as long as you are broke and drained. I stress: **Pray violent prayers** because they didn't come to play.

The Word says our weapons are mighty through God to the pulling down of strongholds. The Holy Spirit which interprets our prayers into Spirit will make our prayers EFFECTIVE... turns our prayers into the desired and needed weapons of warfare. The effective, fervent prayers of the righteous will make much power available to the prayer... and his/her situation. Stay prayed up.

Things like joy, peace, love, blessings, are intangible concepts to us in the physical world, but they are **tangible** things in the spiritual world. Good and bad things can also be transferred, traded, exchanged, and moved around in the spirit world, and also between the realms of the spirit and the physical world.

Things such as joy, peace,-- our virtues and blessings, can be spiritually stolen.

Spiritual power is greater than physical power. God is the greatest power, but if we don't access the realm of Christ and use that power and authority that He has allotted to us, then the lesser, evil, and dark powers may hold sway over the average human --, saved or unsaved.

Get serious, if you are not.

If you are strong spiritually then you are strong in the physical world. But if you are weak spiritually, no matter how bold you may be physically, you are weak. If you're not a stranger to prayer and not a stranger to God, then you have strength in both the spiritual and the physical world.

Things can be moved around and from one realm to another, that is how this works. And exchanged--, there is a thing called evil exchange: virtues can be exchanged. A person's mind or brain can be spiritually *captured* or transferred. For example, a person who was bright, wise, smart and intellectual may suddenly or gradually become a dullard. You may have heard it said, *"He used to be so smart, and very intellectual... we don't know what happened to that boy. He was so smart; what happened to him?"*

Could have been evil exchange. Folks you've got to stay covered in prayer to cover everything from head to toe, both physically and spiritually.

Stolen Parts

If you suspect **evil exchange,** get and stay prayed up, especially for yourself and for your marriage and for the sake of your spouse and children.

Any body part is at risk if you're not prayed up. A person's heart or other body organ can be spiritually transferred, and the person could be having heart problems or a problem with another organ, that on x-rays and tests and scans, there is no medical problem. If this is the case, look at the *emptier spirit* because that's another way to take joy and time from a person and get its victim to spend money.

When those test results come back there will be nothing wrong and the doctor will be perplexed as to why you are there, spending copayment money, spending money, but nothing is wrong. To the medical doctor, it will appear that everything is normal, but you suspect or feel that the organ, for example, is no longer working. This is evil exchange, and it is the result of the *emptiers*.

Things may look like they are normal, but they are not – but you can't prove it because on the scan it is there. Look at the *emptier* because when all those tests come back it will be confirmed that there is nothing wrong with you. Why are you here? You're getting emptied of your money, wealth, prosperity, time, and peace of mind.

For example, a person's **hand** may be spiritually transferred, and the person will not be able to prosper.

A person's leg can be exchanged, or captured spiritually and the person will always be having bad luck. With leg exchanges, the person's marriage will fail. Progress will stop anywhere he enters. This cursed person could even mess up a workplace. Any company he enters could even stop making a profit. That's how bad this is, the violent must and will take this by force. I have seen this live and in person. I may hire a new employee and business goes to heck in a handbasket immediately. If that person doesn't receive the Lord and have a sudden change in their lifestyle and start praying against their evil foundation--, and most often they don't, then I have to suddenly terminate a person I just hired because they are so bad for business. Many times, these folks are deeply embedded in their lifestyle, which they hide in the interview process, but later it starts to show. Many times, their demons, that come from curses on them are deeply embedded in them. Folks, you can't do deliverance on people who do not want deliverance.

When you notice your life going down because of your new associates --, God is trying to tell you something. Witness to them, or get them out of your business.

As scary as this is, and not the subject of this book, even a baby in the womb can be replaced with a different one--, one that is possibly contaminated.

The Earth was made perfect. Man was made perfect; well Adam and Eve, and Jesus were. Everything God makes is right and perfect. 100. The devil comes to steal, kill, and destroy. The *emptiers* can even empty people's life, bodies, their spiritual life, their worship, their prayer life. Get prayed up and stay prayed up.

This is no joking matter. There is no time to sleep, especially while you are vertical, living your everyday *life*. If you are not in Christ, are you, indeed, living?

Emptier Items

One single item of an *emptier* in a house can drain all the peace from it.

Check the things you put on your body, and in your body too, especially your jewelry. If your rings, chains or earrings bear the image of a snake, or a dragon, throw them out. Demonic images in your décor? Get rid of them.

Or if they bear the symbol of a moon or a fish or have eyes in them, or are any demonic symbol, get rid of them. If you have any of the symbols of an *emptier*, you may be inviting it into your life.

Then that opens the door for more demons.

Don't pick up strange things, found things. I never should have picked up that quarter that I found on the sidewalk, and neither should you. Don't pick up anything, and especially don't take them home or put them on your body. No matter where you find them—especially at a funeral, in a cemetery – ANYWHERE. Don't do it. Because you may be bringing home a contact point for an *emptier* or other *monitoring* or *familiar spirit*.

Other people's clothes are spiritually dangerous, unless you know how to pray over everyday items really well. Other people's jewelry. I was guilty of this as I used to LOVE vintage clothing--, but no more.

Women of God—other people's hair, don't do it! I devote an entire section on this in my book, **Astral Projected Spirit Spouse, DIE!**

To the negative, but do you recall in the Bible where Moses' spirit was put on other men so they could help Moses with the work of ministry? Yeah, it's like that but the Holy Spirit was being shared in that case. It's called spiritual transference.

If you don't want other people's *spirits*, don't eat their food, use, or wear their stuff. This is NOT the Holy Spirit that is being shared on these demonic items and food made by evil hands.

You don't want to bring home an *emptier spirit.* They are dangerous, serious and work automatic failure against you until you have nothing.

Sex

Sex is the perfect sin for the *emptiers* to jump into your life.

For every sin, especially sexual sins, there is a *spiritual transaction* that is happening in the background, so, if you have sex with someone – illicit sex, please know your virtue is being taken by the devil because he's somewhere around there. Because if you are sinning, he's there creating a soul tie and an evil covenant. The devil is in every evil soul ties. If this sex is not with your covenanted kingdom spouse, your virtue is being taken.

If this sex is with a demonic personality in the spirit, dream, or with an evil human agent in the natural, whether you know it or not --your virtue will be taken—not might be, **will be taken**. A demonic personality means a *spirit* or an entity such as a spirit spouse, or an evil human agent. The human agent may not even know that they are carrying this *emptier* spirit, or any spirit at all. This evil human agent could be the best date of your life, the most fun person you've ever met. They may not even know they are on assignment. But then again, they might.

I must issue a stern warning here: If an allegedly spiritual person is trying to get with you sexually, and they are supposed to know better, be better, and do better – chances are very good they are not just after sex. You are not so irresistible that they can't help themselves, although I'm sure you're lovely. They are not looking for a new spouse to replace the one they have, they are either gunning for your virtues, your gifts, talents, abilities, your star, or your destiny. **Which one of those are you willing to give up to have sex with somebody else's spouse on the *down low*?**

Hopefully none of the above.

If you think it's just a money transaction, then why do these people bypass sex workers and tempt the innocent or unsuspecting? It's not just because their intended victim is young, it is because their victim still has their star intact, they still have their glory, they still have their Godly gifts, talents, skills, and abilities. The predator is hoping that the intended victim is young enough, dumb enough to fall for his *game*. This old geezer wants to rip those gifts away from that young soul –, male or female.

These old folks **can** afford to pay a sex worker – they don't want the sex worker because all the GLORY is already gone from that temple or street prostitute.

Sex workers: What you are selling is nothing compared to what is being stolen from you. Those few dollars can never pay for Godly virtues and gifts.

Ladies, I'm sure you've met people--, even men who you would never suspect to be jealous of you, but they are. It's as though they want to know what makes you tick, and if they are particularly evil, it seems that they want to dismantle you. It might be subtle, but after some time has gone by you realize that your life is not getting better, it is getting worse. Of course, if it is an illicit, ungodly relationship, what do you expect? The devil can have his way against you if those are the conditions.

That person who wants to break you down, tear you down, dismantle you is after your GLORY. If you have sex with them, that's how glory, stars, and destinies are transferred.

If you've never met one of those, Praise God!

Relationships are like churches, in a sense. If you are in a church and you are being edified, affirmed, built up, experiencing *lift* and life is getting better, glory Hallelujah. But if you are being dragged down and you are lower than you ever were, – even compared to when you first got to that *church*, look closer. It could be that you haven't let go of the world and are trying to play both sides against the middle. You can't do that because a double minded person will get nothing from God.

If you're not fully into God, then the idol *gods* from your father's house, or that you used to serve are coming at you, but if you are not fully in Christ, then you may not be protected against spiritual attacks, such as those of the *emptier*.

Check even closer, if you are okay on both of those issues. Perhaps the church you're in doesn't have any power, or is **not** God's House.

See how we have to always be wise, discerning and on top of things spiritually?

When a person is practicing illicit sex of any kind the *emptier* is having a field day.

Of a fact, a lot of young men's SEED has been taken by and into the marine kingdom. That's when the draining of the glory begins… draining from a man, a woman, a person. The people who are drained, become less and less of himself either all of a sudden or day by day.

I want to give a very particular warning here. I cannot over emphasize getting proper, biblical Christian interpretations of your dreams. If you look up sex in the dream in a worldly book or on a worldly website it will say that is great, that the person you had sex with, you admire, or they admire you and there is some trait or characteristic about that dream sex person that you wanted or wished you had. **Folks this is second heaven, psychic, incorrect dream interpretation.**

But see how it's close, or kind of like what happens. Yes, the *emptier* (whether in the dream or in the natural) sees **YOU** and sees your traits, characteristics, gifts, talents, abilities – your **STAR**, your destiny and it wants those things from you. It wants them before you even realize you have them – this way if you never miss them, you'll never come looking for them. Get Scriptural, Biblical, Christian dream interpretation and prayer-treat your dreams. Talk to the Holy Spirit and ask Him to tell you line by line, scene by scene what happened in your dream and what it means, and how to pray about it. One resource I use is Joshua Orekhie, https://www.youtube.com/@evangelistjoshua .

I know this because when I was young and dumb, I would look in mainstream books and websites for dream interpretation. I was deceived every time. And being told everything is fine, I'd no longer worry about even a troublesome dream and not even pray about it. It's the same as someone telling you everything is fine when they haven't even heard the dream, or the problem yet.

More than one man can testify that he has realized a reversal of favor and good fortune after hooking up with the wrong person. That works for women too; virtue is stolen with illicit, illegal sex.

Later, some may find it difficult to have children when they eventually get married or if already married. Women, it is especially tough or impossible to get pregnant in the natural if you are already pregnant in the spirit from evil spiritual seed from *spirit spouse*. We need Jesus. Get prayed up, stay prayed up and find out where we need deliverance.

It is commonly known among those in deliverance that fibroids are the result of evil spiritual pregnancies and that people who get deliverance for such do not need surgery, but they are healed and are then able to conceive in the natural.

The loss of glory, the stealing and draining of your virtues is a loss of your star and it will drain your finances. This loss of glory makes life a struggle. Not only that, losing your star prevents your destiny helpers from being able to find you. It makes the spouse that God intended for you unable to locate or even see you. It doesn't mean that they can't see you. It means they can't see you as interesting, attractive, or as marriage material or whatever way you or they would describe such a thing. How many women, whether accurate or deceived have said, *That's my husband*, but that person doesn't see her as a wife; they could be, live, work, go to school in the very same place and that man may never even *see* her. That is because of an evil veil, a covering cast, or a loss of glory.

Glory can be lost as we've discussed, and it can be given away by promiscuous living, for example. That is another example of a person destroying their own blessings, life, glory and good things with their own hands. **Yes, men see you as HOT, but as a wife, they see you as NOT.**

While still teenagers, I had a brief conversation with a girl named Doris in my high school expressing my displeasure in how *easy* she was with the boys. She laughed at me and told me to either lighten up, or have some fun. That lifestyle was not for me, even in high school. However, in my own righteousness, I still was wrong. To even have a boyfriend, even one and provide *benefits* to that fellow was also fornication. Am I different than Doris? It's the same sin.

Once you lose your glory, unless you get it back, if you even know that you've lost it, or that you can get it back--, it is still lost. Sin is sin. We must always repent.

We can use the word, *star* interchangeably with glory, because your glory, education, marriage, children, career, wealth are all in your star. Stealing or exchanging of a star doesn't have to wait until high school with illicit sexual encounters. This theft, an *emptier* caper, can be done as early as while the child is still in the womb, at birth or at other rituals or ceremonies related to your child.

There are spiritual predators, empowered by the devil, anointed by the devil. They show up to spiritually vandalize people at events such as weddings, graduations, dedications. Naming ceremonies are not a big thing in the Western world, but you should only let God tell you the **name** of your child, not some random person, not even a relative. Unless you want your child to have the exact life of an ancestor, leave ancestor's names in the past, no matter how happy it makes grandma, grandpa, or the proud pappy.

A star could be stolen but the victim, even the parents or other onlookers may not even know anything happened until much later, and may not even put it together at all, if they don't know WHEN this thing happened, unless the change is instantaneous. It's like so many fairytales we've read where here's a new baby, and here come the witches like Earth is a prison and this is fresh meat. *(Well, the devil is looking to devour, but that is another book.)*

The fact that Herod came running when he saw the star of Jesus Christ having been born is the precedent for this lesson.

Pregnant women, you need to be careful where you go, what you eat or drink and who touches you.

Parents, be careful where you leave your children; who is watching your kids? Don't let it be your enemy. Do not let it be your children's enemies.

And a man's foes shall be they of his own household, (Matthew 10:36)

A friend loveth at all times, And a brother is born for adversity. (Proverbs 17:17)

Parents, have you ever wondered why you're having to break up fights between your kids? Okay, its Scriptural. But watch and teach your own children.

If your child tells you they don't like so and so or going to certain places, listen to them. They may not have the language skills to tell you what you need to hear. If they just say, *I don't like--*, listen to them. Do not let your children's enemies be their babysitters, feeding them, home alone or unguarded with your child. There are spiritual predators out there.

We worry about physical predators, in the natural world, but there are spiritual predators in the spiritual realm who influence and direct evil human agents. Parents, if your child has a sudden, unexpected trauma while under the care of someone, this could be for the purpose of, or the sequelae of stealing their star. The devil loves trauma, and he uses it very stealthily.

Stealing Prayers

The *emptiers* also try to steal your prayers, ruin, and wreck your spiritual life and your connection with God. If you are not connected to God, you cannot get deliverance from the *emptiers*.

Lord, in the Name of Jesus, let all *emptiers* of my destiny and my ministry know that time is up for them.

Herod of my father's house assigned to stop my rising star, or the stars of my children, DIE, in the Name of Jesus.

Every veil or covering cast placed over my life, receive Fire, receive Fire, receive Fire of the Holy Ghost, and be permanently consumed, in Jesus' Name.

Every power under the water and every ancestral serpent that has swallowed my star, vomit it out by the power of the Lord's Christ.

Powers assigned to my life or family, lose your grip, and lose your power, in the Name of Jesus.

Powers of the grave assigned to my life or family, in Jesus' name, *lose* your grip, by Fire. Amen.

In the presence of my enemies, Lord, arise and let them scatter, in Jesus' Name.

Powers that say they will allow me to live a long time, but not prosper--, they need to die, in the Name of Jesus.

Scrambled

The enemy steals children by turning them against their parents, it's as though their minds or thought processes get scrambled. We mentioned the capturing of the brain. The enemy comes for the young, the brightest minds, so stay prayed up and keep your children covered in prayer, whether they go out of the house for school, or you leave them with babysitters for work, always make sure to prayer-cover your child.

Stay prayed up, the *emptiers* are trying to ruin people, doing all sorts of things to folks, including deranging the mind. They can turn folks against you by making them think wrong and weird things about you – things that are untrue. You may not know they are thinking anything weird about you but suddenly relationships or opportunities fall away.

An *emptier* may be casting masquerade dreams. The person who dreamed it is now avoiding you like the plague. This is often done to a destiny helper or someone who will further your career financially. Spirit spouse can do it to natural spouses to drive a wedge into the marriage.

In his book, **Command the Morning 365** https://a.co/d/hyPWlgC author, John Miller prays for the Lord to send divine visitation into the dreams of people who have authority and decision-making power over him and his life. If the enemy is doing the opposite of that, should we not pray against it and also pray for what we would like and need from the Lord? Well, Amen.

In this way, saints of God, do you not see you have to pray far more specifically than a cursory, *Now I lay me down to sleep* prayer at night?

I am uniquely qualified to ask the following questions:

- Do you brush your teeth more in a day than pray? Or, do you pray more in a day than brush your teeth?
- Do you brush your teeth as many times a day as you should?
- Do you pray as often as you can and should in a day?

In the natural, the toothbrushing is important. In every way, prayer is important. Don't slack on either.

Consummate Thieves

Emptiers are consummate, bona fide thieves that they want your money, your *stuff*, your spouse, your marriage, your family. They want anything that makes your life lovely, makes it joyful, anything you really want, that's what they want to take from you. They are like the mafioso, they want your money, you can have all the other stuff. If you don't give them your money, they will take all your other stuff. They may let you live in any state of being; they want money. They don't care if you're sick, but after you lose all your money, you are well, but you are broke. Thieves of darkness are the *emptiers, wasters, swallowers*, and I will add *devourers* to this list.

> For the LORD hath turned away the excellency of Jacob, as the excellency of Israel: for **the emptiers have** emptied them out, and marred their vine branches. (Nahum 2:2)

Reviewing, there are different types of thieves that come to steal from men. The *emptiers* of Nahum 2:2 will allow you to stay alive, but you will lose your money, finances, and opportunities. They will make you a slave. You're still alive, and even working, but BROKE--, emptied out.

The devil knows you can't serve God effectively with no money, no tithes, no offerings, no charity, no alms. You can't be a blessing to anyone. Really, if you can't sustain yourself and your family you'll be a burden rather than a blessing at all, and we are supposed to be blessings. Alive but broke is not the abundant life Jesus came for us to have.

Unbroke, but serving Mammon is also not serving God. Some think because they have money that God is blessing them and will continue to do so. First, where did they get that money? Uh huh. And secondly, if a person is not serving God with their *substance*, then they are not serving God. Yes, I am saying that even if you have money and are not serving the Lord, the devil is okay with you and *may* not mess with you.... well until you end up in hell. There's that.

But then there's the problem of not serving the Lord. Where will your spiritual protection come from when the devil turns on you? Because he will.

Recovery

In order to recover what has been stolen from you, you should know which type of thievery is in operation against you. Being stolen from is an enemy attack, so when the enemy comes in a like a flood, or rolls up on you, you must recognize that and know how to fight back.

As in the natural, if you were filing a police report, know what has been stolen from you. Regarding this spiritual theft, as you file your report with Heaven, what will you tell God, in prayer? Saying, *Help Lord* is a start, but a specific report and prayer will be most beneficial to the resolution of this problem.

How did the thief get in? What's the access point of the thief in your life? How did they get into your life? Is it your own sin, ancestral sin, family iniquity, did an evil human agent send it, or did they come in person and seduce you? Do you have more than one access point that you must close and seal?

Your own sins can condemn you, such as anger, un-forgiveness, carelessness, prayerlessness, or ignorance. It could be ancestral and foundational issues. It could be evil human agents capitalizing on your sin or your family's iniquity bringing curses into your life.

No matter where the curses are coming from, evil attacks are coming at you, and you have to know how to catch the thief and recover your goods. My book, **I Take It Back** devotes the entire volume to recovering all that you've lost and all that has been stolen from you. https://a.co/d/c9sXSwy It especially pinpoints spiritual things that have been stolen and you don't know when they were even taken from you. Many of the following prayer points are adapted from that book.

Prayer Points

Lord any *emptier* that would come for my prayers, let them be arrested in the spirit, and removed, in the Name of Jesus.

Holy Ghost Fire Fall. Fall on these prayers, in the Name of Jesus.

Lord, I command quiet in the spirit; let the rage of any devil, demon, or idol *god* be silenced now, in the Name of Jesus.

Lord, I repent for my own sins, and I renounce sin, and repent for my ancestors back to Adam & Eve, where I retrieve my essence and glory. Amen.

Blood of Jesus, cover me. Remove all iniquity from my life, and my bloodline, in the Name of Jesus.

I bind the *spirit of failure and loss*, in Jesus' Name. I *loose* the *spirit of success* into my life, in the Name of Jesus.

I bind the *spirits of empty hands, empty cupboards, empty bank accounts, insufficiency, and lack,* in the Name of Jesus.

I bind the *spirit of poverty,* and paralyze it, in the Name of Jesus. I *loose* the Power of Wealth, in the Name of Jesus.

I bind the *spirit of chronic infirmity* that drains bank accounts, and steals time, in the Name of Jesus. *I loose the spirit of healing and wholeness, in the Name of Jesus.*

I bind the *spirits of pride, greed, and overspending*, in the Name of Jesus –

especially at holiday time. I loose *spirits of moderation, humility*, and *prudence*, in the Name of Jesus. I loose the *spirit of wise stewardship over finances*, in the Name of Jesus.

I bind the *spirit of rise and fall,* in Jesus' Name. I *loose* stability into my life, in the Name of Jesus, to the Glory of God.

I bind any evil *spirit* that would interfere with my job, education, certificates, diplomas, degrees, licenses, certifications, career, profession and/or business, in the Name of Jesus.

I bind the *spirit of holes in hands*.

I bind the *spirit of holes in pockets.*

I bind the *spirit of foolish spending.*

I bind the *spirit of trickery* as it comes to money, in the Name of Jesus.

I *loose* the Power to get wealth, the Power to receive wealth, the Power to retain wealth, the power to enjoy wealth, in the Name of Jesus.

God, arise and let the *emptiers* be scattered by the power in Jesus' Name. (X7)

Oh God, arise, destroy the work of darkness in my life, in the Name of Jesus.

Wherever I have been emptied, Father, I stand in the authority You have given me to replenish it, restore it, renew it, make it like it was when You first made it, in Jesus' Name.

My stolen virtues, hear the Word of the Lord, come back now, in Jesus' Name.

Wicked powers behind barrenness, miscarriages and unfruitfulness in my life, of any kind, receive Fire, in Jesus' Name.

Any evil person or power turning my children or helpers against me, receive the judgment of Fire, in Jesus' Name.

Any evil person or power trying to steal from my children, their star, their virtues, receive the Thunder Fire of God and let your powers fail, and be exposed, in the Name of Jesus.

Any coven or evil altar where I, or my family are being called for destruction, scatter by Fire, in Jesus' Name. .

I decree: destiny *emptiers*, your time is up, DIE in the Name of Jesus.

Emptier of my glory, or my spouse's glory, or my children's glory, your time is up, die, in the Name of Jesus.

Emptier of my favor, or my spouse's favor, or my children's favor, your time is up, die, in the Name of Jesus.

Emptier of my pockets or bank accounts, your time is up, die, in the Name of Jesus.

O Lord of Mercy, by Your Mercy, restore to me everything that the *emptiers* have stolen from me, in the Name of Jesus. (X3) Amen.

Whosoever is using my glory to shine in the spiritual realm, may they receive constant, relentless, and ever-increasing Fire until they release my glory, in Jesus' Name! (X5)

God arise in Your power and disgrace my enemies by Fire. (X3)

God arise in Your power and disgrace the emptiers by Fire, in Jesus' Name.

Any spiritual cage that refuses to let me go, in the Name of Jesus, break!

Coven powers mocking my prayers, or mocking God, die, in Jesus' Name.

I bind and paralyze the *spirit* of the *emptier* in my life, in the Name of Jesus.

Lord, build a wall of Fire, a hedge of Fire, and a mountain of Fire around me, protect me from the *emptier*, in the Name of Jesus.

I paralyze the powers of the *emptier* over the works of my hands, in Jesus' Name.

I will enjoy the fruits of my labor. My God gives me the power to get wealth, to receive, and enjoy wealth, in the Name of Jesus.

You, *emptiers* and *wasters* release me now, in the Name of Jesus.

I command all evil *emptiers* to *lose* your hold upon my life, lose your hold against my marriage, my family, and my business, in the Name of Jesus.

Emptiers and wasters working to make me lose out spiritually and physically, cease & desist, in the Name of Jesus.

Power of the *emptier*, you will not empty my life, in the Name of Jesus.

Power of the *emptier*, you will not empty my marriage, in the Name of Jesus.

Power of the *emptier* you will not empty my business, in the Name of Jesus.

Power of the *emptier*, you will not empty my purpose, in the Name of Jesus.

Power of the *emptier*, you will not empty my destiny, in the Name of Jesus.

Power of the *emptier*, you will not empty my ministry, in the Name of Jesus.

Power of the *emptier*, you will not empty my career, in the Name of Jesus.

Power of the *emptier*, you will not empty my family, in the Name of Jesus.

Power of the *emptier*, you will not empty my children, in the Name of Jesus.

Power of the *emptier*, you will not empty my life, in the Name of Jesus.

Power of the *emptier*, you will not empty my health, in the Name of Jesus.

Power of the *emptier*, you will not empty my finances, in the Name of Jesus.

Power of the *emptier*, you will not empty my Peace, in the Name of Jesus.

Power of the *emptier*, you will not empty my Joy, in the Name of Jesus.

Power of the *emptier*, you will not empty my happiness in the Holy Ghost, in the Name of Jesus.

The powers that emptied my mother and emptied my father, that emptied my ancestors and planning to empty me; Lord forbid: Lord Jesus rebuke them, in the Name of Jesus.

Emptier of my father's house, <u>die</u>, in the Name of Jesus.

Emptiers of Time, be scattered, Lord, redeem the time, restore the years, for me, in the Name of Jesus.

Any *emptier* planning to tie me down to one spot or in a job that is not part of my purpose or destiny, die and let me go NOW, in the Name of Jesus.

Lord, restore to me everything that the palmer worm, the cankerworm and the locusts have eaten, in the Name of Jesus.

Every satanic warehouse, where my goods, my wealth, and my riches are, by the Hand of God and His mighty angels, I take it back, I take it back, I take it all back, in the Name of Jesus.

I take my Kingdom spouse, in Jesus' Name, for Kingdom purposes and that my joy will be full.

I take my children—born and unborn, in the Name of Jesus.

Lord, reverse every evil done to my life, my spouse, and my children. Restore, renew, replenish us, in Jesus' Name.

I take back my career, in Jesus' Name.

I take back my education, my diplomas, and certificates, in the Name of Jesus.

I take back my business, in Jesus' Name.

I take back my ideas, in Jesus' Name.

I take back my successes, in the Name of Jesus.

I take back my ministry, in Jesus' Name.

I take back my joy, in Jesus' Name.

I take back my peace, in the Name of Jesus.

I take back my blessings, in the Name of Jesus.

I take it all back, I take it all back, I take it all back by the power in the Blood of Jesus.

I take it all back, in the Name of Jesus.

Spiritual warehouses, Satanic warehouses where they have my destiny, my wealth, my riches. I bind the strongman in the Name of Jesus. Angels of God, remove the strongmen from the doors and gates in the Name of Jesus.

> The LORD will restore the splendor of Jacob like the splendor of Israel, though destroyers have laid them waste and have ruined their vines.
> (Nahum 2:2 NIV)

Lord, restore my authority – which is awesome in You, in the Name of Jesus.

Lord, restore my identity, and all that's been stolen, in Jesus' Name.

Father, we know that in our proper authority and position, with the Holy Spirit, as Adam and Eve had before they sinned, as Jesus had, being a Perfect Man. Jesus said what He can do, you may do also, even greater things, because He goes to the Father. We have the authority to REPLENISH our lives, our Garden, our part of the Earth that we are to have dominion over.

As long as we are upright before God, and in Christ, in the Name of Jesus.

Thank You, Lord, for restoring the splendor of Jacob like the splendor of Israel, even though we may have suffered at the hand of *emptiers*. Thank You for restoring us again, in Jesus' Name.

I seal these declarations across every realm, every age, every dimension, every timeline, past present and future to infinity, in the Name of Jesus.

Any backlash because of these prayers and this Word, backfire 7X, in the Name of Jesus.

Dear Reader

May the Lord bless you richly and deliver you from every thief of darkness, especially the *emptier*. May your life be full of all the good things the Lord intended that you have. May you finish well and be a blessing to your family and your entire bloodline.

In the Name of Jesus.

Amen.

Dr. Marlene Miles

Other books by this author

AK: The Adventures of the Agape Kid
AMONG SOME THIEVES
Ancestral Powers
Barrenness, *Prayers Against*
Battlefield of Marriage, *The*
Beauty Curses, *Warfare Prayers Against*
Behave
Blindsided: *Has the Old Man Bewitched You?*
https://a.co/d/5O2fLLR
Churchzilla, The Wanna-Be, Supposed-to-be Bride of Christ

Collective Captivity, *Break Free From*

Courts of Marriage: Prayers for Marriage in the Courts of Heaven (prayerbook)

Courtroom Warfare @ Midnight (prayerbook)

Curses of Blind Men

Demonic Cobwebs (prayerbook)

Demonic Time Bombs

Demons Hate Questions

Devil Loves Trauma, *The*

Devil Weapons: Unforgiveness, Bitterness,...

The Devourers: *Thieves of Darkness* (Book 4)

Do Not Swear by the Moon

Don't Refuse Me, Lord (4 book series)

Dream Defilement

The Emptiers: *Thieves of Darkness* (Book 1)

Every Evil Bird

Evil Touch

Failed Assignment

Family Token (*forthcoming*)

Fantasy Spirit Spouse

FAT Demons (The): *Breaking Demonic Curses*

The Fold (5 book series)

    The Fold (Book 1)

    Name Your Seed (Book 2)

    The Poor Attitudes of Money (3)

    Do Not Orphan Your Seed (4)

    For the Sake of the Gospel (5)

Fruit of the Womb:

Gates of Thanksgiving

Gathered

got HEALING? Verses for Life

got LOVE? Verses for Life

got HOPE? Verses for Life

got money?

How to Dental Assist

How to Dental Assit2: Be Productive, Not Wasteful

I Take It Back

Legacy

Let Me Have A Dollar's Worth

Level the Playing Field

Living for the NOW of God

Lose My Location https://a.co/d/crD6mV9

Man Safari, *The*

Marriage Ed. Rules of Engagement & Marriage

Made Perfect in Love

Money Hunters: Beware of Those

Motherboard (The) - soul prosperity series

Name Your Seed

Occupy: *Until I Return*

Plantation Souls

Players Gonna Play

Power Money: Nine Times the Tithe

The Power of Wealth *(forthcoming)*

Powers Above

Marriage Ed.: Rules of Engagement & Marriage

Mulberry Tree, *The* https://a.co/d/6JP7KqK

Seasons of Grief

Seasons of Waiting

Seasons of War

Second Marriage, Third~~, Any Marriage

Sift You Like Wheat

Spirits of Death, Hell & the Grave, Pass Over Me and My House

Soul Prosperity soul prosperity series 3

https://a.co/d/5p8YvCN

Souls Captivity soul prosperity series 2

The Spirit of Poverty

StarStruck

SUNBLOCK

The Swallowers: Thieves of Darkness (Book 3)

Take It Back https://a.co/d/dZnVE25

This Is NOT That: How to Keep Demons from Coming at You

Throne of Grace: Courtroom Prayer

Time Is of the Essence

Too Many Wives: *Why You Have Lady Problems*

Tormenting Spirits
https://a.co/d/dAogEJf

Toxic Souls

Triangular Power *(series)*

    Powers Above

    SUNBLOCK

    Do Not Swear by the Moon

    STARSTRUCK

Uncontested Doom

Unguarded House, *The*

Unseen Life, *The* (forthcoming)

Upgrade: How to Get Out of Survival Mode

    Toxic Souls (Book 2 of series)

    Legacy (Book 3 of series)

Warfare Prayer Against Beauty Curses

Warfare Prayer Against Poverty

The Wasters: Thieves of Darkness (Book 2)

What Have You to Declare? What Do You Have With You from Where You've Been?

When I Was A Child, I Prayed As a Child

When the Devourer is Rebuked

The Wilderness Romance https://a.co/d/jfkMlnj

- The Social Wilderness
- The Sexual Wilderness
- The Spiritual Wilderness

The Wilderness Romance series is not a romance novel series. These books are about relationships with people who are still in the Wilderness, how to avoid them, or what to do if you've married one.

Series:

The Fold (a series on Godly finances)
https://a.co/d/4hz3unj

Soul Prosperity Series https://a.co/d/bz2M42q

Thieves of Darkness series

Triangular Powers https://a.co/d/aUCjAWC

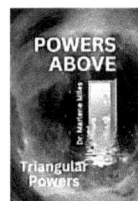   

Upgrade (series) *How to Get Out of Survival Mode* https://a.co/d/aTERhX0

www.ingramcontent.com/pod-product-compliance
Lightning Source LLC
LaVergne TN
LVHW021405080426
835508LV00020B/2472